The Midlands

The Midlands

Tony Williams

ISBN: 978-0-9927589-3-6

Cover photograph © Eleanor Bennett
www.eleanorleonnebennett.zenfolio.com

First published July 2014 by:

Nine Arches Press
PO Box 6269
Rugby
CV21 9NL

www.ninearchespress.com

Printed in Britain by:

imprintdigital.net
Seychelles Farm,
Upton Pyne,
Exeter
EX5 5HY
www.imprintdigital.net

The Midlands

Tony Williams

Nine
Arches
Press

Tony Williams grew up in Matlock in Derbyshire and now lives in Northumberland. His first collection *The Corner of Arundel Lane and Charles Street* was shortlisted for the Aldeburgh, Portico and Michael Murphy Prizes, and *All the Rooms of Uncle's Head* was a Poetry Book Society Pamphlet Choice. He also writes prose fiction. *The Midlands* is his second collection of poetry.

CONTENTS

To Mam, Dad and Tom

THE MIDLANDS

The Midlands are crying, crying for haslet and bacon,
    crying for bridges where railways falter,
crying for sumpters no longer needed
    on towpaths of moss and built-upon pasture
and troughs of time-stilling water
    where rodents and litter are drowning
in mushy-pea visions of Methodist churches
    and hedges and car keys and crisps.
They are crying for conkers and tennis balls lost in the woods,
    for mortgage advisors, for money itself
to the price of one pint of their sulphuric bitter,
    which also they cry for and cry for at length in the night.

They cry in the car parks of aerodromes, deep in the cellars
    of buildings that used to be bookshops.
They cry over fences, at steam-engine rallies.
    They cry over dogs and bags of granulated sugar.
They cry for the rugby posts lost in the mist,
    for vandalised road signs and nullified Sundays,
for teenage perceptions of dreadful pan-Midlands despair
    at the doom of solitude made real in bedrooms
invaded by older sisters themselves driven mad
    by the tussocky desert of pop songs and taciturn lads
in the suburb-like towns and town-like suburbs
    of Dirgeville, and Grieflington, and Sad-at-Heart.

Here is neither one thing nor the other.
    There is no one waiting at the level crossing.
There is not the flash of headlights on the wall
    to say that someone loved is coming home.

There is not even clarity and rage, but only
      rain setting in on a plain between ridges,
the magistrates courts as busy as ever,
      the chorus of starlings chattering trenchantly on
in the skies, an unfound grave of a Mercian king
      under wurzels, new housing, and out-of-town Asdas
that mop up the rheum of the foothills
      that lean-to the North.

HALF-DAY CLOSING

Is the station unmanned? The taxis
won't answer, so make your way up
to the verge and the bus stop, and wait
by the grave of the can of Vimto
for the Tardis to take you and drop you
outside the dark face of the library
in the windy and desolate town.
Feel underfoot the tilt of the paving,
hear its clink, and the gurgle of manholes
covered with burnished discs like the biscuits
you can't buy in the awningless grocer's.
The cash machine works but there's nowhere
to spend it. The butcher's, the florist's,
the hardware shop, all are abandoned,
the café, the caff and the chippy, the lido.
The pub will re-open at six.
The Spar is the corporate scab of the high street
with deals on the merlot should Eastwood
ride into town with a thirst for the shy
and melancholy set. (You're not Eastwood.)
They spurn it, the townsfolk, the merlot,
the striplights. The traders are gone
to the back rooms of their dreams,
the upstairs flats where they mainline heroin
or sit at the screen and order Meccano on eBay
or mosey on down to the meadow with mother's
old copies of Erle Stanley Gardner,
dancing their fingers across the invisible strings
of violas and cellos, baking fruit pies
and releasing healed otters, blowing glass,

sifting pre-Roman remains, sleeping with lovers.
As the sun breaks through its low angle
at what would be closing, they turn their eyes
as one to the far unprofitable West, and pray
to the god of not-only-Sunday
for loose ends and turning the sign, and fine weather
all the way down to the bend in the river,
always like this with the fridges switched off
for the rest of their half-days.

The OK Diner

It's fine, but it's not Little Chef,
the diner where we stop for lunch,
not Grantham, or Stamford, but the Newark branch
(not in New Jersey but the prairie state of Notts).
The coffee is bad as bad coffee
and the tea is worse. The burgers
admittedly make good the promise,
the American Dream of the mouth,
but where is the salad? What is the meaning of 'salad',
here in Ohio-on-Trent? And who
when they heard 'mayonnaise' thought to mix
a spoonful of whipped cream with a tub of St. Ivel Gold
kept back through disconsolate years
in order to assault and teach our tongues?
It's not been discontinued after all: the half-arsed A1
running by past the window to Retford and Donny,
to Wetherby, Stevenage, Spalding and Corby,
the lead-brick vestigial towns; airfields and water;
the stain of oil in the car park and fencing
that staves off the field where the donkeys sit down in protest
at rust as the answer and essence of all journeys' ends.
Even her accent, the waitress whose presence makes up
not at all for the absence of service – her accent is there,
and makes up for it all, as she explains
that she cannot say if the guacamole contains tomato
because she does not know what guacamole is
except that it's green. Her accent redeems it,
the lunch in the wilderness, bored and unclear
as our Logos was destined to be. We listen,

halfway up the country and home,
halfway between Hertford and Alnwick,
to the guileless twang of a voice
on the blunt edge of England: muttering on
by the side of the national abeyance
for as long as the priestess has left of her shift,
in love with Burt Reynolds and his sidekick Curly Fries,
at last and in deep and on tap and unable to curb
the sarcasm that lames our dreams.

THE COWS

Here are the cows and I love them.
They move from one field to another
and in every field they dance
to cow music I cannot hear
in steps I do not understand:
now grouping to graze in a corner,
one standing alone as a sentry,
now suddenly migrating, now
reaching the shape of an emblem
spaced out on the pasture
all facing the same way,
utterly still. Sometimes
they break through the fence to lay claim
to the lane and the grass of the roadside,
which placates them – cow freedom
ends here. I love them,
the cows and their constancy,
here every summer all summer
to munch and proceed at the pace
of the hoof on the sod in the sombre
grass-ceilidhs of their cow-religion.
O feast of movement; O flexing
knot of flesh like a fist or a heart;
O sacred hugging of herd;
O slow kaleidoscope
whose shifting field shows
all colours and atoms belong
in all constellations, and are cow.

THE PATH THAT FOLLOWS THE TRAVELLER

'It is not my intention to be illiberal'
    – Wordsworth, *Letter to the Bishop of Llandaff*

The rain is proof. The rain offers
baptism to those who would fulfil
their responsibilities as gardeners, as dog-walkers,
as students of the terms on which one man
might cross the land without salary or retinue.

Only when your felt hat melts, when you taste
salt on the face's shore, and a thorn wind,
do horizons sink behind the mist
to take in continents. I mean cold solitude
taught you togetherness. And the rain grew your beans,
each brown brain soaked in northwesterlies
until pod parliaments of foetuses
began to greenly form and wait.

In the rain you grew old. Let those who preen
and pine to die immaculate
mock your tiredness,
your bracken beaten down by rain recanting.
You turned to firesides and silk to soothe
your shrivelled old been-in-the-rain-too-long
fingertips. To have stayed where you were
was against Nature.

All travelling goes somewhere, turning
away from the once-beheld sublime,
out of the valley of light towards the grave,
towards the glass grave of fame
and so much water that even
the umbilical cord of your signature risks
dissolution like the stone of your beloved hills.
It is enough that you passed through,
snapping umbellifers as you went, to show the way,
leaving little lakes in the prints of your boots.

DERWENT

'the fairest of all rivers'
                    – Wordsworth, *The Prelude*

They are not one, the river in the crook
of my elbow and in yours. The shallows
are not, the reeds, the shawl of brilliant green
weeds are not one, nor the stepping stones
leading submerged to the far shore.
There is a reason rivers share their names,
but it is not that the rivers are one. Each river
is its own region happening again:

upstream are the paintworks and the canoeing gates,
then the high ground of another moor.
Downstream is private fishing and, beyond
the wide-smiling weir, an idle brick mill
no longer part of the river's argument.
This river hidden in the shadow of the cliffs,
swollen by others running under stone,
cannot imagine another stone and another hill.

Listen: and you will hear the quiet bank,
the still downfall of democratic rain,
discursive murmurs which a listening child
might hear as the silver progress of a stream
because the stream is there, where the child
is playing while the adults sit and talk.
It is the sound of movement watching
the leaves that fall and fall through time.

Be suspicious of what the river teaches:
brown water cannot be throttled or sued,
and lovers can't be blamed for why we love them.
It is the godhead's delta, one as many
are one, like an edition of a newspaper
(the *Angling Times*!). Its headline
is a gurgling message which you alone can hear.
Listen to what the stream is calling, asking –

lie back in the meadow. Maybe in water's dozing
you will drown, unable to respond.
That will not matter. Others will hear
the river's calm involuntary seething,
and they will answer the challenge you have failed.
They will fail it too. That does not matter:
there are others coming, always themselves and listening, running,
rivers returning to the open and generous sea.

THE RURAL CITIZEN

'You took our buses, now give us some footpaths'
    – headline in the *Northumberland Gazette*

Scorning the honey-pot mountain with car park and centre
where local crafts are displayed and distinctive
patterns of rock that have 'shaped the life of the valley'
are shown colour-coded, scorning the barely visible
hump of the wall of the Iron Age fort
(now a khazi for sheep) and the cup and ring scars,
I emptied the flask in the river, dropped off my rucksack
as shrine on the roadside, buried my boots
in the mud by the gate where mud-coloured cows
had thronged to be fed or to die since enclosure,
and set off in trainers and jeans for the commonplace hill.
There was the shell of the old-fashioned telly
dumped in the layby, litter from Starbucks,
the four hundred yards on the verge of the sixty-zone road,
the overgrown stile to the field with the bull in,
leading to nowhere in woods where eerily echoed
the cry of a buzzard being mobbed by black-coated crows.
Easy to think of the buzzard as me, the crows
as the agents of death. Easy to shiver and think
that my boots might rise from the earth and pursue me,
assisted by footprints in that mucilaginous mud by the gate
and herds of the cattle as solid as mist on the fields
at morning, as cow-breath, the ghosts of the drovers and driven
coming to claim me. But truer that I was a crow,
one of the many, the buzzard the gold-coloured State
that was conjured and breasted by money – its infinite,
intricate feathers. We pursued it, I and the ghosts

who did not walk with me, could not, marooned
in their estates and parishes, interred in the graveyards
and kitchens and pubs by immovable earth
and the price of petrol and frailty of reasons for leaving
the heated and taxed habitations to go
across country, and learn by the ache in their knees
each swell of the fields that contained them, each darkened corner
where nothing but dock and the odd sprig of rape
could be found to enlighten their hearts on the topic of growth.
I was the lesser, the rural citizen
who does not understand his city
which hedgerows and tied-shut gates refuse him.
We dream of the desert, for the desert's monstrous
sculptures make plain a horror we hope stands with us,
the hosts of the dead that make of the living a host
and underwrite our demand to the sacrificial king:
you have taken our first-born sons, you have taken
our right to guard every hearth with a spear;
now give us the ear of the scribes of the law
that asserts us, now give us, by royal command,
our being in the fields of wheat, and the beasts.

'BUT TELL ME, WHO ARE THEY, THESE TRAVELLERS?'

(Rilke)

Who drop a trail of litter so
that landowners will see and know
that misfits, spectres, trouble, coughs
have moved through what is cordoned off,
like footprints on the virgin shore.
Who are not here any more,
who hang the moles on barbs as proof
of vagrant, muddy-trousered truth.
Whose names are thus: *unknown, unknown.*
Whose flesh outlasts the store of bone
in certain lights and certain songs.
Who leave their condoms blossoming
among the cowslips all around.
Who are not lost and can't be found.
Who gouge the fields like the swine.
Who broke the branch and drew a line
through every page of statute law.
Who happened to be there, and saw
a cheap arrest get made, and laughed.
Who burned the harvest of the croft
and spilled the pail, like infantry
in the ugly rush of victory
lit by the glories of the west,
and freed the young, and shot the rest.
Who daub their lords with axle grease.
Who carry languages and fleas
from one shy district to the next
and take the birch and scree as text

to render pallid by their route
the parishes of wordless light.
The whisper of their feet in grass
says, 'Now cartographers will pass
and close the landscape of the clouds
to tell where you are not allowed.'
Who carry human skulls inscribed
with wonderment. Who bribed
the watchman with a knife to sleep
and fudge the total of his sheep.
Who are the servants of their dogs
and daily sacrifice their legs
in honour of the makeshift hearth
and narratives that only start.
Who loiter in the quarry and
repeat less sweetly their demands:
the adolescents they impressed
grow colder when they get undressed.
Or maybe this is all a lie
dreamed up by bigots on the fly
for fear that outlaw movement might
unfix the boundaries of right.
Who sit and menace on the gate.
The cross of whose crusade is not
to die but passing through to leave
and reappear, some believe,
in halo on the hill that marks
the far extent of royal parks,
and by their leaving, show the folk
that those who think of coming back
are always and already home,
while those who carry in the palm

no coin stamped with somewhere's king
prevent a stillness happening
to make a grave of valley towns.
They minister beyond the manse,
enabling locals whom they meet
to feel great tides may loosen yet
and by their talk of fen and ditch,
help those villagers to reach
the ceaseless, tram-infested streets
of cities, new and obsolete.

PARK WITH BENCH AND STATUE

Sap had dropped from the trees
and covered the head and face
of a statue of Love in the park.
Pigeonshit streaked with dark
was the pinstripe in his suit.
The sap was sticky and sweet.

Two flies flew by that face
then settled down for a taste,
each on the blank wall
of an eye, and while
those gloss-black pupils sat
tasting the rot of the sap

the statue learned to look
at an empty bench in the park.
The statue stood and cried
under the trees and stared
till the flies went back to the wind
leaving the eyes stone blind.

'THE WHOLE CITY... OPEN'D ITSELF TO LOVE'

(Sterne)

Cars kissed in the jams. Their engines throbbed
and the drivers exchanged photographs and chewing gum,
and lent each other phones to call their lovers.
Confetti fell from the trees. Graffiti said, as ever,
Hayley takes it and *I love Ricky by Hannah.*
School too went on much as it had before
but there was no end to playtime, and nobody
lost their lunch money or grazed their knees.
Laughter shone boxed in rows in the terraces
and stacked, reaching to heaven, in tower blocks,
and the boozers and bozos at bus stops
ran through the parks looking for injured strays
which they laid on the leather seats of saloons
pulled up on the kerb while the solicitors
knelt, giving away their clothes and gadgets.
In the football stadium, at the ice rink,
at the post office not yet closed, in the cafes,
there was sharing of sandwiches, there was eye contact,
there was hand down the front of a stranger's pants
in full view of everyone. There was modesty,
there was the tenderness of All Together. Everyone surged off
like a drunken mob to the much-loved bridge
and threw their money into the brown, indifferent river.
Traffic wardens left saucy notes
under wipers. Firemen stood, watching dogs
stuck in the act of copulation, applauding.
The alleyways shook with the sound of bouncers weeping.
(The man in the CCTV monitoring suite also wiped away a tear.)

And in the law courts everyone was acquitted, everyone confessed,
everyone forgave and everyone was forgiven,
the judge sentenced himself to an afternoon off
and the usher bought ice creams for the defendants' children.
The mayor skipped along the high street refusing bribes,
and the citizens went on stacking shelves, cleaning offices,
queuing in the job centre, singing the more cheerful hits of Elvis
and Kylie Minogue. There was a wet kiss of rain.
I had my jacket zipped up and my cap pulled down
and walked through the streets with my hands in my pockets
among the waltzing couples
thinking of you so far away
and whether you'd received my letter
and smelt the scent on the envelope.

A BOUQUET FOR PAULINE VIARDOT

It is not 1843, the premiere of *Lucia* bursting forth
in Petersburg, the dawning of her lucid Russian day,
Chopin still alive, composing preludes
in honour of the smell of the earth
and the sight of bare trees against the opal sky
in the carriage, very early in the morning;
the numberless, unnecessary, splendid parades,
the Second Empire still to come; and Eugene,
breathless, drunk, the belt of his greatcoat hanging down,
dancing along the bank of the Neva to her song.

It's 1859, she's back in Paris singing *Euridice* by Gluck,
who's dead, as Chopin is dead and gone:
she thinks of him, remembers a drawing of a human brain,
sitting in the shadow of an ornate clock,
in a dark room full of costly clutter,
with high ceilings, waiting to go on,
waiting for the men to come with their flowers,
their doffed hats and invitations to dine.

She manages a little scale under her breath,
the glass clouds, and Eugene in Russia
thinks of her – perhaps it was a phrase from that little
      consumptive waif,
that canary, the songbird in her yellow dress,
above the clatter of the tables – and turns on his heel.
Michael – did I ever tell you – what about a little game of faro –
first, let's eat! They'll set us out a table – Viardot –
the singer – a whole month I was in love,
on the strength of one performance which she gave!
The lamplight smears and shines across crystal

in a voice-filled hall, a man frowns tuning his cello,
while she in the gloom swallows the silence with a smile,
moving her hand towards an impossible chord.

Late elevations of tone, a key-change,
an impresario, spreading his hands wide,
something in his face physically strange,
and the sound of a scuffle in the street outside:
hare with gooseberry sauce – pig's feet –
a rattled old woman clearing her throat –
another three bottles of champagne –
the Empire's stars and the sharp horizon
and the cigar's smoke troubling my heart.
A woodcutter drove by on an empty cart
as I sat on the wall of the wharf –
but I'm repeating myself. Turning up in a phalanx of
    swells and whores
(those rooms where high society reaches round to its tail)
– raised glasses, voices, downcast eyes – whirls and spills –
hands of cards, quarrels, assignations – all
of it in movement, all of it unclear.

And her, Viardot who will outlive Victoria,
a waxen image of calm in the tremulous room,
dispensing a glance on the footmen, the silverware,
thinking of the first line in a song and the difficult rhyme.
Fortunes capsizing: the dreadful, sleepless faces, the
    picking up of chairs,
the chimes of yesterday – exits, the big stampede.
Settling a debt with a retired officer of guards
while his comrade strokes a tart's hair
who lies softly weeping, and that fat little author
murdering the language with his tongue
– that's the accompaniment to her song.

No one hears it but me. The closed door, the ebony panels,
    the gilt
and the tall, sad windows and the brindle cat –
the fire resplendent in its vast proscenium
blushing its last bow to the empty room –
her pearly hands moving listlessly over the lacquer
and the brilliant, remorseless keys – she sings to herself
softly and no one hears it, not I, Eugene, so far away across
all the indignant, superannuated bishoprics, sending her roses
like all the other roses – and another – and another –
chess and peppermint tea, the smell of leather,
a horse's nose distorted in a lustrous tuba –
swamps and stern forestations, water rails,
partridge, snipe, woodcock and grouse,
juvenile storks and God knows what else,
tortoiseshell, alabaster, tuberculosis...

Enfin, a snowdrift of last thoughts, those flower-angled brooches,
though we are very far from the end – boas
and scientific breakthroughs, Frenchmen
writing indecent books, attempting the Matterhorn –
private theatres, manic-depressive maids,
pet names for minerals, rhodomontade
as a way of being – rum and soda water, syrup of quince –
these to Madame Viardot with my compliments.

ANASTASIA

I had at first thought she was Ingrid Bergman
whose 'Nordic freshness and vitality'
might undo a murder by pressure of beauty,
a Slavic Eurydice scarred with the wound of Achilles
as proof of her blessing. But there's only a *shvibzik*,
a chit of an imp in the mist of St Petersburg's marshes
and Lili (or Ilsa, or Anna), the lady-in-waiting
to welcome her lady home to the living,
with Grandma descending the staircase
on the arm of a prince and declaring,
'Go home,' to our mannish and barely imagining gaze.

Here, at the gate of the house, or the madhouse,
or graveyard (a pit by the side of the road),
here's Papa, or Laszlo, or Lorre,
or the rest of the family, dead in custody,
too late for 'the breaker of chains' to redeem them
through mysterious youth and herself in the hospital,
Fräulein Unbekannt, the object of wish and of pity,
the lost of the Romanovs, frantic, 'not her'
and gone to America, taking old Europe
along with her 'lapdog and heavy valise'.

O how on Wikipedia we look for her, we sleep
on hard cots without pillows, we hosts of impostors
wishing that history concerned only personal circles
which we could in dreams come to know and be part of,
be 'royal'; we give up the letters of passage
to leave with the ones we really love, we click on the pictures:
a young girl sitting at a white piano, doing her knitting, asquint
at the edge of a frozen lake, naive, as the clumsy photographer
lets his own shadow intrude on her lap as he shoots.

THE GLASS PARTITION

i.m. Arnold Bennett

It's true – I'm having ardent thoughts
about late Victorians – the yellow silks and camisoles,
the grand skirts, petals of a monstrous rose,
wristlets of lace and the modest flounce,
the stays and the primped hats and the hair pinned up.
Pulled tight. The small, pale hands
and the porcelain voice talking of ornithology,
cloudless in spite of the shop's wooden echoes,
and 'that house' (Italianate), and the cost of upholstery.

It is the great age of decoration.
And I'm the gawky clerk, safe in his corner office,
watching the shop's light flatter the black
bulb of my father's hat laid there on the desk,
among the elaborate reckonings of the ledgers.
Everything is bound in heavy fabric.
Light casts her eyes down through the glass
partition, but does not speak to me.
Dust and phantoms move beyond it.
I rest my chin on the dado. The smell of beeswax
mingles with the fumes of a winter lozenge.

The glass is the schema of a lunatic.
A commerce glints across its city of bevels and frosts.
My large eye meets a rhombus,
whose clarity is to show
a mustard aura round her avatar:
it is the shape of her shapes, the pattern. And,

catching the light on its way from the fusty sky
is the oval of lawn, old emerald
in an ironwork setting
                      – she ran across
in her stockinged feet, in the dusk of the suburbs,
and the door was open and the lamps shone out,
but the elms shook overhead in the gathering dark
and I knelt in the gravel and laid her dropped brooch
on the doorstep, and went away.

There is the scrape-and-tinkle of the little bell
(the door, or a tram shuttling by on the street).
She goes. I watch the shadows recede
through the cubicle's judas, and would fly to her,
and kiss her, and die for her, and strike her down
with all my modern power and brass, astronomical precision.

LAURA, A SEAMSTRESS

I've fallen in love with a mole.
The way they was talking, stood round,
      me in my dress. So I ran,
pushing the teasel suitors back
      till I found the place
the man was shovelling daylight down,
slid down myself, and there:
      my little man.

A thimbleful of cider is a lot
for a girl like me. I'm perfectly serious.
It's cramped, of course. The dark sugar
      and nutmegs, the blue
      larvae, see-throughy babies.
The roots of the trees make me think of wallpaper,
but what wallpaper I've ever seen's
      so mad with spirals?

His name is Wudower. He carries a silver watch,
each tick a mole-year. When he dies
I will still be a girl, I'll do
      I-don't-know-what.
He knows I'm laughing at him.

I eat all the slugs he brings.
My eyes change colour, my teeth
      feel like someone else's.
His little snout
      braises in my hot spittle;
I put my finger in his side
and his back paw thumps in reflex.
      A purse in my hand.
      Podgy. Slumbersome.
He can keep his waistcoat on when he enters me.

JACK WOOLLEY'S DREAM

i.m. Arnold Peters

In bed he listens to the radio:
the sound effects of Schmallenberg and five-bar gates,
unscripted chatter in The Bull.
Thou art a veal calf in the cellar's dark.
Thou art thy spouse's cousin. Glasses please.

Faceless Kareninas frolic naked there
with moody Grundys in the barn of the ear,
the boring county of all day in bed,
too sick to read. No one can visit now.
What keeps it closed is how the valleys lie

and roads drift off in silent snow to choke
the afternoon as with a maypole ribbon.
All this is the invention of a mind
which needs a playground for its childhood:
he in Grey Gables dreams Grey Gables real.

The town is thirsty for a dearth of time
and static's lull. There are antiques sobbing.
Tom's new sausage vies with burning Grace.
It is the vale of lengthening shadow, the bridge
which takes each soul beyond its Am.

MEMOIR

Chief amongst us was the Patch of Dusk,
     oblong of midges and departing teal,
sweet melancholy A4 sump of woodsmoke
     and roosting pigeons
and the cocktail hour: shadows of gunmen on the scree,
     sparrows dressed as yellowhammers,
shuffle of an old bear approaching
     with white burrs stuck on his dark-blue coat.

We paid a shifty obeisance, bowing low
     with soft flesh where we ought,
as automata brought in to praise, to be brass.
     Our friend the Watermill clapped slowly,
grinding the fields' seed between her thighs.
     The Jackpot with All Holds puked out with its
       rhythmical crash
all our days, and a grid of coloured bulbs
     ennobled the equivocal looks we gave to see
it was always paid in tokens, and each day dawned
     a 99p breakfast in the empty pubs of Whitley Bay
and the empty beaches stung by wind and rain,
     the gloom-green shingle,
carsick growl of the penniless, hungover youth
     a long way from home.

Why should we speak?
     We breathed in air of the Curve of a Slope,
polished the tree roots of that parish
     and dined on individual shepherd's pies in
       stoneware pots.

I made little pencil sketches and rolled dice
        to see who would give the black spot to the Patch.
The snow continued to fall. Mam sang along *tra-la* and I
        raced toy cars on the theme of loyalty,
never considering that it might be me,
        Eel Climbing Up a Ladder,
cover image of wartime-reissued John Buchan,
        hat concealing the egg of an osprey,
lying down here under the purple clouds
        among the remorseless spindly legs of the heather,
listening to the shouts and barks of the king's men
        and the *shunk shunk* of their muskets and rucksacks
and muskrats, and the *fish* of their fine calves
        through cocksfoot wet with the dew of evening.

Fox prints

We lunched on fur.
We lunched on daytime TV
    and the crushed stems of delphiniums.
We lunched on youthful wonder and misery.

We lunched on *that's as you please* and *not in my name.*
We lunched on *cherchez la femme* and *es geht um die Wurst.*
We lunched on our wits and the dark motives of strangers,
    on pain of death, which brought bite to it,
    in the rain and began to like it.

All the while sitting on extruded plastic.
It turned out that the girl I had kissed
    was a bust in *ciment fondu*
    and I had still not recovered from the acid.

We lunched as the bells rang out the dawn of *anno domini*
    fourteen hundred and twenty-seven.
We lunched on the dust this performance disturbed.
It had suddenly struck us that our shin-bones and thigh-bones
    were not so different from the ungulate
    kebabs we had been gnawing
    so many centuries. We lunched on self-pity.

There was not much we thought unlunchable –
    fox prints, road tax, the contents of drip trays.

We lunched in fear of the pizza-cutter which Maureen
  had sharpened
    through the long nights of her down-there
     inflammation.

A lot of notes were written around that time,
     a lot of phone calls made without niceties. Cake
     cannot fix
     everything.

We lunched, and the gals in the war room mapped our progress.
We lunched, and *albeit* sprang into my head almost immediately.

We lunched, wretchedly, watching the vein of the man
     who had rented us our cutlery
     throbbing.
We lunched, sometimes, and sometimes did not.
The scratch of the tartan rug on our skin was annoying but so
     was the man in a frock coat bellowing
     Goethe out across the lake.
We lunched, limbless, in the starlight.

We lunched on the implacable and saw
     a destiny, of sorts, unroll before us.
We lunched on exoskeletons.
We lunched on towards evening and plotted
     a spot of brunch for tomorrow.
The clouds could not give us the answers
     whereas the dinner table could.

We lunched until our lips bled and the blood
     congealed and glued them together to strike us dumb.
We lunched until the darkening hills came alive
     with the sound of government forces
     spraying us with ideology,
till the heads of the drowned
     bobbing across the Dove
     scared the kingfisher from his perch.

Dear Rhino, love from Hippo

With skin like ours, my friend, the usual
        insults of a rivalry descend
        harmlessly as confetti
        or the blossom of trees
        we rub our backs against.
Nor would expressions of sympathy survive
        the foul tempers of our readership. Instead
I'm sending you this chatty letter, a crocodilian
        sickle of courtesy in the poisoned soup,
        which might worry you if crocodiles did.
Be assured of my continued indifference.

In the past month
        I have eaten a rare fly, a wristwatch,
        a silhouette, odd chunks of my rivals' chins
        and a vast tonnage of hay which you,
dense hoover of the midday sun, missed
        when the eternal salad drawer of the night
        clanked open as you slept. Or are you
        nocturnal too? It's hard to see in the dark.

You doomed swordsman, me cloven-hoofed
        and cackling like a whale. You unicorn,
        me Cadillac bumping up
        against the blonde girl's legs.
Whatever happened
        to your ambition to become a freelance illustrator?
Every time I pass the hospital
        done out like the concourse of an old European station
        with the pediments high up based, unattributed,
        on your sketch of an elephant's toenails

I think *dommage!* and of the royalties we'd claim
        if ever I'd passed my law exams and you
           weren't such a raging and wretchedly cantankerous drunk.
At least we don't owe money to the giraffes.

You, engraving from the days of the plague,
        me poster paints printed by a dipped-in bum.

Listen, priapus-face, I've been
        divining the future in the map of illness
        disclosed in my own used nappy.
I think you'd enjoy a cheese and pickle sandwich
        if you dared to enter a deli. I think the jackals would swoon
        like spinach wilting if only you'd show them The Dance.
I've been listening to local radio over the internet.
        I've bid on a doll's house and
        a signed photo of Lothar Matthäus.
I've heard a grown man singing falsetto
        for the amusement of chumps.

Thanks very much for the library card. I've read of
        isotopes, anarchists, artistic foibles of heretical sects.
I've read a few classics, and enjoyed your waspish annotations.
        (I dreamed I saw your initials
        carved into the brickwork of the Bradford Alhambra
        but didn't inform the police.)

You tin opener, me turtle without a shell,
        you me, me you. How long
        will we put up with being haunted
        by the ghosts of all the antelopes
        mistaking us for mobile crypts to hole up in?
Now that I've developed the transmogrifier
        we could go anywhere, do anything –

spend a century as a standard lamp, become amoebas
in the eye-sockets of a monkey, seek election.
So don't get pettish. Sling your keys in the bowl.
We'll put our heads together, become a
hiprhiponopocetarosmus,
get a scholarship to university, mend a motorbike,
step out one morning after a pot of tea,
carrying a cudgel, thinking
how the sky's colour reminds us of approaching evening,
how the deaths of our loved ones will become
as fey a topic as essential oils and the history of the
Anabaptist Church
which we might tease open with a little sullen laugh
just to see if it hurts
over a tall glass of Pernod.

THE LUCKIEST MAN IN THE WORLD

A Shetland pony stood on my foot,
an event of great mildness and illumination –
even the pinching pain folded under
the quaint sense that such a thing had occurred.

It happened in the May-time, when the coat's
half on half off your back. I waited half an hour
in the hospital, and then to bed
with a glass of barley water and a cloth-bound book.

I could not read so scoffed co-codamol and slept.
I cancelled my appointments and the world,
previously tottering, did not fall.
My foot hurt, but was joined to my ankle, so there it stayed.

For the rest of the month it bore a yellow bruise,
a dandelion next to a silver birch.
I limped a bit, when I remembered to do so,
till that blaze of silliness turned to ash and dispersed.

So what if I cannot wear my best shoes?
I am not after all standing for the regional assembly.
Could there be a greater good fortune than to have
a very small horse tread on the top of your foot?

THE PHOTOCOPIER

Perhaps you assumed that an hour would be enough –
you're not, after all, Johannes Gensfleisch zur Laden zum
     Gutenberg,
and only want two sides of the minutes from last time and
how our working practices may be made more efficient.
There are jobs queued up like tankers on Teesside's
grey and unmoving horizon. There are buttons behind panels.
There is a smell of burning. You have forgotten the code,
you are out of paper, of staples, of toner, of patience
and when the noise comes to tell you the bastard is jammed
you reach in to the hedge to pluck at a tight and pristine rose
as if snow and silence in Eden is what you're assaulting in
     wanting
one each of this miserable sheet for the meeting.
You are up to your elbows, a general surgeon of Daleks,
turning knob A clockwise and wondering how panel E
might be opened, whether this catch should be flipped
up or under and why the number to call for the engineer
has been Tipp-exed over. People arrive and ask
'if you have a lot to do' and you must not savagely answer 'yes!'
In the time you are waiting, stuck on copy 16 out of 20,
your colleagues turn up to microwave lunches, read memos,
get promoted past you, get married, have babies, die.
Your clothing passes from fashion, and from the annals of fashion.
The forests they plant to redeem the wood for the paper
evolve into swamps, are compacted and end up extracted as oil
to fuel the cars that you see passing by
as you stare out the window, the fourth floor's calcareous Sphinx,

at a Nile of rainwater sluicing its way to the gutter,
at the car park barrier rising and falling
like the pole which the ferryman uses to punt
souls luckier than yours across the forgetful river
as passers-by shuffle one after another
who all look somehow the same, as if municipal zombies
were spewing *ex nihil* at x clones per long and unsalvable minute
from a mouth of the gadget you cannot access, with blank
unoriginal eyes made up into shadows with kohl
manufactured from toner that cannot be fetched from the
    stockroom
(read: 'Sanctum of Ghroth') till lunchtime tomorrow.
Necrosis afflicts your most cherished nostalgia.
You watch the dust lying down with the paperclip.
You know there will be days and days like this.

LISTENING

I didn't mean to overhear
the scrape of chair legs on the floor
and sour breath of the bored, enshadowed janitor
nor how he conflabbed on the stairs
(it echoed in the squarish well)
with an ingrate from HR, how you
were falling basementwards, towards
the ferret-sprainted woods where mats
of needles deadened steps and skulls
of foxes, badgers, falcons, bats and shrews
emerged like eggshells of the news.
I heard the round of sirens in the night,
the airless click of satellites.
I heard the muffle and the timely knock,
the seconds jerking round the clock,
lonely and insomniac,
the sound of no one coming back
to fill and free the lock. I heard
a drunk man shouting COCK
and shrunken voices answering No,
his loiter in the orange yard
and how he turned to go
against a wind that breathed your name.
I heard the water cooler's hiccup send
a bubble of the future up,
an iciness to be my friend,
and how beyond the traffic's burr
your cough performed a Pyrenees of grief
upon a screen – as I was dropping off – I heard,
between the dog barks and the Word of God,

a vixen's scalp-contracting scream.
I heard the silence of the room.
I saw the silence of the moon.

CONTINUATION

'He knew it, and for the time quite welcomed it,
as a continuation, but didn't know what it continued'
   – Henry James

From one farm to another,
footpaths, partridges breaking cover,
a funny-looking stump between fields of rape,
power lines, a cleaned-up animal trap,
the old brick of a kitchen garden keeping me out,
clags of clay on my boots...
Cessnas and airsocks, the enormous
fields of the east coast to cross
and always the promise, but never
the cool score-in of a sluggish river...
I reached the front door: no answer.
Cobwebs and stonedust in the groove
and seam and glossed edge of panel,
lock plate, architrave;
a cracked porcelain sign. I went round
to the courtyard, past the piggery (converted)
and the glasshouse (a furniture
restoration workshop) to find
a man on the back step taking off
a pair of light-guzzling gloves,
leather, black in the sunlight, black
in the cool of that cloister's calm.
I feared their permission for hard tasks.
He threw them on the step,
took my hand in a warm palm.
I missed what he said as you miss what's said in dreams;

I was trying to think what the gloves meant. Already
somebody was opening a bottle and the rooks
winked in the sharp treetops behind the house.
The long buzzsaw whine in the workshop began its stint.

STONE PIGSTIES

That's how it was
            that's how
that's the beech leaf
            frosted down
on the corner of a road
            nobody travels by
nobody travels
            that's how a bang on the head smells
or looking into the sun at teatime
            a bang on the head
through the black lace of the trees
            on the ridge behind the house
teatime on the ridge
            that's the sodden path
the leaf frosted down
            to the ruined farm
with its stone pigsties
            and ton upon ton of quivering mud
with last year's grass
            going bald above it
the teatime of the farm
            and a bang on the ridge
corner windows
            swallowing the light
holly berries
            dropping down
into the depths of the brambles
            where nobody can find them
frosted down
            on the road

in the mud
     travelling by
that's how the sodden it is
     that's the path and how
at the quivering of black lace
     the head in the trees
turning at teatime
     swallows itself the light
banging the window
     going bald
the tearfulness of the sun at teatime
     on the ridge of the nose

THE SHADOW OF ARMS AND LEGS

It happens whenever I reach
        to open a certain door
or kiss the sofa's back
        with my hip as I go past
the way of moving stirs
        and I remember *me*
the shadow of arms and legs
        continually sneaks
behind the brain to go
        towards the house before
the secret knot of routes
        by the cliff and farm
to aerial masts on the moor
        and the quarry behind a fence
to the fields of pasture's slopes
        the crow-smutted copse
and the marginal corpse
        and hush the smoke-filled sky
where stories might sketch in
        a ground no longer there
to the cold air to the smoke
        from the chimney and the path
down through morning dew
        to the back door of the house
to snails and expiring mortar
        wherever its crumbs may fall
where I will never arrive
        but love to worry and grieve
how we walked across
        in the years before the years

began to unravel the light
        the snow before snow
and the bramble fruit
        bled beyond purple

THE VELVET TABLECLOTH

She's sitting down at the velvet-covered table,
bronze-yellow, lion-bronze-red-yellow
(the table stands on a lion's carven claws),
tasselled stringily and the velvet loose
like close-cut, dead and yellowed grass.
It seems you could draw your finger through it
and leave a sign to be read, tomorrow,
by your grouchy, put-upon, lethargic descendants –
a sign of the wisdom you're full of now,
and the wine you're full of, but princely too.

Being drunk, all you can do is to drag your palm
back and forth across the nap of the velvet,
amongst the glasses, in a space you've cleared
of ashtrays and dinner plates. She's listening to you,
you're impressive, you pour you both another slosh of wine
but you know you won't get to sleep with her – so,
the velvet tablecloth is a pet, a friendly cat
to deflect and absorb your frustrations,
what you can't or she won't let you say.

You stroke it. You arrange playing cards on its surface
and watch how they raft on its illusion of flatness.
She's sympathetic – what could be worse? You're tired.
You're both tired, and the booze is wearing off.
You don't say: *I remember this tablecloth*
from when I was a child. She hasn't deserved that.

THE STEALING OF WILD CAT TOR

'he became his admirers'
   – Auden

The cliff has been stolen.
They dust the scene
with the cliff's own dust
and learn the cliff was taken
by a giant who, for fingerprints,
has an old and wrinkled face;
and every smiling dab,
if you listen close,
exhales a smiling whisper
in that old man's voice:

examine this region:
how narrow the space
crouching behind a sheep-pen
trembling he takes
the nights, the railway arches
cavernous, lofty as
the smokeless hill
common to us all
to throw away the key
all along the valley
settle in some cave
a faultless love
as he left them there
the sour and shiftless water
(it dissolves in water)
sulk no more
imagining my grave

THE CLOCK IN THE HALL

The place was one of sudden drops,
great lumps of grit, and fields, and gaps
where rivers channelled out their way;
and in one gap, a village lay
between the cliff and river where
the fossils slowly swam, and stared
across the gorge to see a house
perched on the edge of that abyss,
a stone ship icebound in the green
ocean of the Pleistocene.
The cargo in its earthly hull
was the lost brain of an empty skull:
a tall house on an oblong plan
designed by some clear-thinking man,
its rooms lay round a shaft of air
so that the centre wasn't there
but offered up a void to grant
us room for object and event.
A tender person, or a fool,
could wind their life around that spool,
a knot to pick and ravel out
a core of mystery and doubt.

My bedroom nestled in the roof,
a shelter which conserved the love
ascending by the stairwell's flue,
and thus I delicately grew
above a chasm, and although
I was inclined to vertigo,

I liked to stand and bask, unseen,
on the top landing, where I'd lean
over the banisters, looking down
at pot plants, shoes, the telephone,
the bald spots of my male kin
and how the sunlight filtered in
from windows on all sides; but most
greedily I admired the dust
(which drifts in every open home)
accumulating on the helm
of a clock, grandfatherly and tall,
the hallway's wooden sentinel.

Brass finials crowned the little spire
and on the half, and quarter hour,
the small bell tolled for minutes that
had lived their three-score seconds out
while lower down, inside the tomb,
an always-swinging pendulum
described the scoring through of days
and how the daily-darkened skies
absorbed the progress of a moon
austere and patient as a nun.
It had an owl-face of surprise
with winding-holes in place of eyes
whose involuntary will to see
the one and only tragedy
observed the passage of our lives,
all that blesses and that grieves,
with sharp hands drawn across that face
alike in horror as in grace;
and its indifference, its calm

centre to our living storm
made me a private temple there
at the far bottom of the stairs,
a long, unwinding metal fact
caught in a wooden cataract
to counterbalance, step by step,
our tumble headlong down the steep
wave that rushed away from there,
the still arrest and source of care.
And if you asked me for the noise
I'd want to drum me through my days
and on into the dark, I'd vote
for the breathless clearing of the throat
the mechanism would perform
ahead of every hour's term:
a whispered, minuteless *Salaam*,
more comforting than any psalm,
that ushered in a fanfare blast
to give that present to the past.

Those two decades of keeping watch
have ended, but the moments stretch
the lost interior of peace
beyond co-ordinates of place
and time. The pleasure and distress
of adulthood, the fudge and mess
I travel with, are held in check
by conjuring that oubliette
where wound-up instruments of mind
can let the universe unwind.
I surface in the racing tide
which may be fleetingly defied
by imagining a chime

that seems to stall, while keeping time,
and reel the hours back; or I'm
a child still staring at the clock,
imagining a future shock
from my high eyrie's reverie,
an opposite of memory
indulged in childhood's sickness-dream,
safe from passion and from harm.
It makes no difference which is real,
the child or the grown-up. I'll
be shivering above the drop
of that domestic telescope,
until the hill collapses and
the house subsides from where I stand
to leave a phantom in the sky
transfixed and waiting there to die,
the sentinel to stir and shake
and all the final time to strike.
Eternity will end like this.

The house should blush, because I kiss
the heart inside its empty chest
where dust and my remainders rest,
layer upon layer of
the shed skins of a lifetime's love,
a kind of meditative grave
or piggy bank where I can save
the homeless and nostalgic host
of solitudes that make my ghost –
a fixed afflatus of the stairs
which scorns all going anywhere.
O bring me ham and lemonade;
I'm in the sanctum where I stayed

(or say a cell if you prefer)
alone through every day and year –
so bring me playing cards, and books,
young women with suggestive looks,
bring arguments and new machines,
a plastic bag of runner beans
and half a pint of London gin;
and hammer till I let you in,
give you my hand and take your coat,
then cut your other-worldly throat
so that your entrance does not scare
the clock from its distracted stare –
and out of time, our corpses might
escape the total of its sight.

JUST A LATE VISIT

Halfway up a hillside
scaring off the crows
strewn across the carpark
kicking through the leaves
cold at hand
where he came before
opening a window
looking at the village
speaking to the air

he kilters by the railing
high above the river
finds the hotel open
stands at the bar
gazing at her arms
flex the bitter out
what he hasn't said
catching no one's eye
the sound of other voices
muffled through a door
he forgets to listen
looking at the paint

boots slip on the stones
dropping down the bank
beyond the mossy church
near the tufa cave
he grasps the ferns in handfuls

to keep his footing there
traffic fumes and rumbling
from a little distance
here the single-storey
premises are locked
the gutter lying open
taking things away
where the wall is aching
no one there to kiss
here was always waiting
always here for this

past the small house
edges through a stile
the half-sunk boat
tadpoles like shadows
swimming to the sides
the wet gravel slides
as he walks across
the empty carpark
carrying a net
cars beside the river
someone going up
gruff and nodding greeting
more than enough

the tufa fountain
stagnant foam of rock
clouds of midges
specking on his throat
water in his boots
leaking on the paving
lifted from the water

the slime is flat and cold
weed that blew like hair
in its own country
thus he mourns its loss
leans against a gravestone
in place of love
the family here

draining his glass
the lizard-tail latch
of the window he stood at
half his life before
and always since
dizzily emerging
from the hotel bar
the slope of the gable
catching on the cobbles
lightness moving over
perfume or laughter
follows on the path
knowing how it goes
he turns and glares
hard across the valley
home among the dead
this damp afternoon
fish across the cobbles
where the bucket spilt
dying in the air

THE SNAIL OF MASSON

Run around the hill
looking for the snail
streaking out its metal

tracks across the rock –
spittle where a spark
might survive the murk.

Help me look for it –
straight into the night,
pulling on your coat

and bring your glass, never
let the drink be over
I share with you, brother –

listen in the lanes
for the wheel that turns,
playing all the tunes

that haunt these slopes.
Haul the silver ropes,
touch them to your lips

to taste the slow career
and dromedary ore
of another living there

shivering in a place
where to find and to lose
blesses every pace.

Help me, then, run out,
find the little foot
that slides on loot

by the paths that curl
a mirror of the whorl
round the treasured hill.

We could flag it down –
ask it in the dawn
what these scribbles mean:

emblems of the shell
freight what mineral
solutions of the real?

Or does hell's sellotape
spell by sly ellipse
a curse of earth's collapse:

each footfall through the crust
to sound the starless worst,
echo, and be lost?

UNDER MASSON

I heard the rain falling on the canopy above me
and an echo of the dog once lost on the hillside
barking accusation from the musty cave's back,
so I moved towards it, beyond the valley's light:
down into the socket of the small cliff's face,
past that house of rock and the litter of those who stayed there,
loitering in the rain: in towards the memory
that Masson is and thinks. I shivered down its throat.

Down at the lake that sniggered under pasture
I watched figures running along the glistening shore,
lit by burning torches fixed to the rock.
Teams of the dead, spry and stunted children,
the dead-tired old, slaved to shift and heft
the iron-wheeled pulleys to handle up the statue
towards its pedestal, a statue of the figure
standing in the keister of a scull on the water
sternly shouting orders through a horn of brass.

Gasping now, I paddled, naked as an earthworm,
out across the lake – closer to the dinghy,
closer to the rockface, closer to the statue
raising its head to stare at the dead ones
whose dreams sustained it wrenching at the wet ropes,
retching now and then. As the monstrous statue,
water dripping down, light catching crystals
in the water-carven brow, raised its monstrous face
to look across the cavern, the hill's thoughtless heart
mined of all feeling, it saw me there

in the still and sleeping water and knew at last
that only my breathing, my trespass in the dark,
voiced the damp director, gave it to itself
and raised up the stone.

Then the statue tumbled.
The scull began to founder. All the figures ran.
I made it to the stone shore as the torches died.
I lay and listened to a whisper shake the hill:
Leave him there, who searches for the searcher.
Shadows fall on nothing. Water cannot stay.
Let him always listen to animate the voices
and glean some metal from the tired earth.
Let him gather coins, but let him never dare
to open his hand and read the empty palm.
Let the hill erode. Its stone will be his tomb.

Then the wind died. A stone-fall of agony
drenched my shattered thigh. I had escaped from movement.
Dark had followed light. I listened to the chime
of water-droplets falling echo in the nave,
the long song building pillars of stone
to hold the rooted roof of the hill's great dome.
I listened, now, and waited for the dog to come,
the dog that I'd been chasing to come and lick my hand.

THE DECORATOR

The original enamel bath had been ripped out.
I clattered my step-ladder up to the top floor,
where the landing was narrower,
and met the ghost of a boy who lived up there.
He was the one who'd carved Greek letters
into the polystyrene tiles of the roof
with a shatterproof ruler. He showed me
the various rooms. I heard voices.
In the airing cupboard a housemaid's corpse,
his sweetheart, had turned to grave wax
in the humid air, a perfect doll
but for a bad patch on her side
which had the look and feel of a Bakewell pudding.
They whispered. Their childish voices
framed the calm sentences of adults,
but I couldn't get the gist. So I turned on the radio.
All day, fresh brews, fags out the skylight,
trying to ignore the unquiet spirits in the corner.
I thought of ringing in to Jeremy Vine.
I found myself humming nursery rhymes.
The wallpaper had pasted back the years,
and when one patch the size of my fist
showed in torn layers the colours of a chaffinch,
I sat on the edge of the jacuzzi and wept.

Something Dreadful

The caver trapped inside the cave
by rockfalls gets to test his grave
a day or two before he dies,
and though it ruins the surprise,
at least he'll make himself at home
by clawing at the stony dome
to scratch an epitaph of blood –
My fingers were not any good –
then weigh the pitch of his last words,
though these will not, alas, be heard.

Above, the calcite stratosphere,
both massive and absurdly near,
displays a sea of stars of quartz
to mitigate macabre thoughts
while all around the stagnant air
constricts his limitless despair
until the dread and blue disease
constructs euphoric fantasies
of airy rooms in palace towers
where chess and tisane stretch the hours,
the white cities of Provence
and clever princesses who once,
unfolding those eternal limbs…
But these are merely vulgar dreams.
The cooped-up kobold shortly knows
a buried truth that all suppose:
you are alone for ever more
inside a room without a door.
He warms his house in the abyss

with spurts of fear-compulsive piss
as all the endless minutes loom,
an only child in a womb
so jealous of its foetus that
its wall contractions do not let
but close and keep forever clenched
its darling, nil-potentialed mensch.

This live transition into death
(as babies live before their birth)
shows living has a furious strength
in spilling out beyond its length
and knowledge of the yet-to-come
is just a loan on future harm,
a mess of pottage for the farm
he'll buy with torso, legs and arms
and mind and brain. His is the fate
of knowing early that it's late,
and he can soon enough expect
like Frisian harvest-king, or Pict,
his execution in a ditch
below the stunted groves of birch,
lit by a guttering torch and gone
in hat and rope to please the corn
with belly full of final meal
to close the circle of the wheel.

The corpse-to-be lies in the hall.
It is a lying-in of state:
break out the wine and silver plate.
The meanest fissured rock can be a
maharajah's mausoleum:
the closing of a life should scare

the living to adorn the air
with worshipful superlatives.
But nothing at his bidding moves;
it is as private as a dream,
the cadence of his soundproofed scream.
The grave-goods, Kendal mint cake, nuts,
his body and his leather boots
will spoil and soften in their shell,
the hollow and unfriendly hill.
He passes through, he passes through
the sump of language, me, and you,
of memory, and even grief:
an insect baked inside a loaf
inside an oven in a house
abandoned to the raging grass
and lurid atoms which lay waste
across a universe erased.

THE MINE-ROADS

Going down Clifton Road, I see the yellow bulbs
burning through fanlights in the glossy doors
and dream whole households back to frigid life.
Or see the silhouette of a stile in a cow's eye,
myself a dim figure at the bottom of the shaft.

*

There is a village underneath the village.
The mine-roads even made a city,
if industry and darkness are what make a city,
and like an ancient city-state were flooded
by a river, and abandoned long ago.

*

Dark streets, lit by what quartz eyes
have held of passing candlelight,
cross unconjoined with the sunny lanes of home.
The ground of home contains more names
than murmur in my heart's gazetteer.

*

And when I step towards the public bar
I pace Black Ox; lost in the woods I follow Moletrap Rake.
The dog-walk round the hill takes me across
Silt Rake, to Jacob's Dream, and down
to Groaning Tor. But never home.

*

These passageways disopened by the light
insist on being there, on leading down
through lack of light, through earth and rock
towards a nameless pool. They crave the breath
with which I speak of them. My skull.

*

Walking the mine-town's graves I wake them,
sending a shiver down each ditch
on the narrow-gauge rails. There's no one there
to feel the permaslime on rope-grooved walls
or taste lead ore in the wet air; but a footstep
hears itself, echoing, in the dark.

WELSH DRESSER IN THE OLD HOUSE

Sometimes I sit alone.
The kettle peaks and dies
to leave the vinyl hiss
of a speechless hour –
how I admire
the boring radio
but have to switch it off
to coax the boredom on
to ripen to the kiss
of gentle emptiness.

*

To see the silver daylight
shine across veneer
and feel the air
sigh throughout the house
as a small fire sends
a thread of violet ink
up towards the sky
is charm enough to take me
to the dresser there
where I lay and smelt
the carpetful of dust.
My palm knows the bulb-
of-garlic feet better
than I know my numbers
or the names of those I love.

*

How dark the wood
in whose landscape splays
the thistle and the fruit,
the chevroned field carved
for a dead and unknown knight
who lies, a spread body there
at the rustling of the wheat,
and by a rose is pinned,
whose story I was told
but cannot bring to mind.

*

Every nick and scrape
in the rain-gilt wood
of my grandfather's face
has pressed itself deep,
is what my fingers are,
and far behind my eye
is the mirror and the plates,
the left-there ornaments
and rammel in the drawers:
playing cards and notes
to meet at the dance,
the box and crocked kazoo,
the hoarded buttons,
no siblings at hand
to share the stories with
of bulls loose on the road
or a girl-scented coat.

*

So it looms towards
words which I could speak
if a visitor came,
except the cantrap breaks
whenever others come.
There's no one on the steps
at night some years ago
and someone with my face
in an old-fashioned suit
surveys the shrubs
at the Whitworth dance,
the black of unlit glass
and an empty room
whose key may well be lost
in the lockless tangy drift
in the dresser's depths.
It's a lifetime's work,
how the dresser takes
the rooms of all its years
to heart and locks
its dancing dumb,
to loosen now and then
for someone sitting still
in a listening house.

THE INVISIBLE MANSE

a rispetto

The road here more or less follows the river,
but the final curve before the town
was once a deeper, more definite corner,
till the road was widened – as, a half mile on,
the cliffs at Scarthin Nick were blasted
to make more room for Fifties traffic.
Here no cliff was wasted but the wave washed hence
a Methodist Chapel and its manse.

Cuboid, heavy, many-windowed
as the mills, sharp black and grey
in the sun and warm-stone-shadowed
on a busy and interminable weekday,
it sits immovable as a deity's will, loose-tiled and shabby.
Nothing now but a faint bend on the road to Derby,
it opens straight off the street if you have the key to the door.
The looping wires carry lost telegrams by that ear.

In the photograph none of the windows
lets us see the girl staring out or hear
the minister her father's calmly commanding voice:
'World be as you are.'
She wears a dress above her ache, an onyx brooch.
She has seen a fox on the far side of the river, endured reproach
imagined from her father's mouth. The new coal men,
Italian immigrants, Catholics but hardly at all, have moved on

with their coal and their singing.
Nothing now is as loud as the river.
Her frightful He is the arena of her longing.
His Nay is the ground of the Yea of her lover.
I think if I go there at night when the moon's
cloud-covered, I will not see the manse
in the dark and its absence. But if I stand
under the road sign in the cold tunnel of wind

that chaperones the river, I'll smell the mud
and hear as she lies with a hand on her brooch her whisper
through the clack of branches in the woods,
'Is the devil real?' – which only the devil can answer.
I must wait for the moon to see her,
would need a telescope to understand her fear,
but there where she found no shelter but the house's stone
I find no stone but shelter, and the road sign.

I think of her fingers counting out the pence
for tradesmen; my great-grandfather's grave
up the road in the churchyard of the Anglicans;
her voice and accent tearful, yes, and grave;
bird's nests perched halfway up Wild Cat Tor;
horse carts, prewar lorries; British power.
She hides away and watches the hard
efficiency of the redcoat mill, and blushes at its argot.

I have descried her in the murk of the pool
under the always-smashing glass knuckle of the weir,
and she is listening to her father rehearsing his spiel,
thinking meanwhile of the grinning poacher
who waved to her watching from the house's cover,
the devout woman and the travelling preacher,
and what room, if they called when her father was out,
she would receive them in to listen, never to let

go but always to keep living there the voices talking
that pluck and smooth at her fretful ease.
This is presence: a fish's eye, a lost gewgaw, nothing,
a sick, scared girl hidden in a dark house,
not daring to light a fire, faithful but worried,
humming the 'Rock of Ages' for courage,
feeling with power enough to persist in the clean air
of death, the wider road, more or less here.

ARRIVAL

'You know the way to the place where I am going'
          – John 14:4

You're almost where you started, passing by
the ruin in the woods, damp wreaths of fires
that cheered the world before the world dispersed,
pub-shadow of not-so-recent kisses
wiped clean by the always returning rain –
approach the woodside and the closing garage,
the hill beginning to stink in its clothes of slate.
The town is nearly empty. You have waited
too long, thinking this is destination
which really is the doorstep of your road.

Imagine coastal farms and city buses,
the villages which shoulder off their light,
sharing no meals with those just passing through,
and moors whose heat and stories of forgetting
you cross for the last time, going down
from the sky and from the bilberry in fruit.
Desire twines the fingers of the stream.
You leap it. It pursues you down the valley
past fields of clay-red, placid cows
and the placid bull. Speak to the friendly hedges.

Step slowly inwards to their secret language,
hands held open. Swallow the grave orations
your mother tongue's too late for. These are the brick
arches of reneging lovers, the children
playing in a garden you don't know:
the shining green tent of the runners buzzing
on the slope by the stern senatorial trees.
You have learned nothing. Here, by the railing,
you listened. Both you and your brother betrayed us.
Now your fragile wings are drying in the air.

Lullaby

O my son,
do not let me hear of the death that awaits you.
Do not let me see you arrive
at the white city, whose gates
record the story of your deeds
and love, the famous tragedy: her face
already at the window, grieving.

Your walking should disdain
the burn of years behind it in the road.
Here is the sky-attempting moor.
The heather grows back soon,
and you may go there where the flames
have half-erased what once was me and mine,
but must not linger.

Already you are trembling at the sea,
a feast of light below you in the bay
where trade the ships of unknown majesty.
May you receive the news in irritation,
on the road, too busy for sorrow.
My silence is beside you in the hedge.
Go on without me, wielding your sword of fire. Go.

THE TOWNS HAVE BURNED

The towns have burned, but we don't know they've burned.
The prowling oligarchs spew sulphur and deceit
from side to side along the blackened road.

One preens his talons in the air and crows,
'I own the lamplight and the flames of gold
and you may shelter in the shadows there.'

Towers of settled ash approximate
the guild halls and the terraced streets
and yards and pubs and rows of graves so well

it almost seems that we could lay our flowers, cry,
or speak at meetings and be heard. Except
we reach and touch them and they fall

in clouds of cinders which have lost all light
but scorch the grass for everyone to know
what beasts have passed and how they made it burn.

But we are human still. We'll gather up
a store of rubble and the will to build,
and work, directed by a show of hands,

so that in spite of living at the end of days,
or seeming to, the fact shall stand:
the children of our children shall have towns.

ACKNOWLEDGEMENTS

Thanks are owed to the editors of the following publications, in which some of these poems first appeared:

English: The Journal of the English Association
Magma
Material
Poetry Review
Shoestring
Their Colours & Their Forms: Artists' Responses to Wordsworth (Wordsworth Trust)
In Your Own Time: The Northern Poetry Workshop Anthology (Shoestring)
Double Bill (Red Squirrel Press)
For Rhino in a Shrinking World (Poets Printery)

Many of these poems were written as part of a research fellowship funded by the Arts & Humanities Research Council [grant number AH/J007706/1], for which I'm extremely grateful.